JOGGING MCDOWELL

DISCOVERING CHICAGOLAND WILDERNESS

Les MacLean

To order additional copies of this book, contact:
Xlibris
1-888-795-4274
www.Xlibris.com
Orders@Xlibris.com

Jogging McDowell

Discovering Chicagoland Wilderness

I wish to speak a word for Nature, for absolute freedom and wildness, as contrasted with a freedom and culture merely civil——to regard man as an inhabitant, or a part and parcel of Nature, rather than a member of society.

Henry David Thoreau

"He loved Nature when loving nature wasn't cool"

JOGGING McDOWELL

DISCOVERING
CHICAGOLAND
WILDERNESS

In fond memory of my father in God's Word,
Dr. Victor Paul Wierwille,
And my parents, Dr. and Mrs. Malcolm S. Maclean, Jr.

In loving dedication to my immediate family: sister Sandy Mana,
brother-in-law Luigi Manca, niece Nora Manca Wickman,
nephew-in-law Neil Wickman, great niece Eowyn Wickman

Close Friends: The Hoth Family; Julie, John, Jessica, Logan,
Sasha, Mallory
The Fries Family; Abrah, Ted, Elle, Jude, Renee and Hal Henderson

TABLE OF CONTENTS

FOREWORD

I wish to thank my sister, Sandy, for introducing me to McDowell Woods. My first time, there, was when she took me hiking one late afternoon after I woke up from working a graveyard shift. It was late summer in the year 2000, and I had been living in Naperville for less than a year. For most of the 1990s, I was working long summer seasons in Montana's Glacier National Park and winters at western ski resorts. My thoughts, and heart, were still in pristine wild country with grizzly bears, moose, bighorn sheep, and elk in my backyard and a backdrop of white-threaded mountains, aspen foothills, and flower-strewn prairies. I had also been used to vast rolling prairies coming to life with antelope and prairie dogs. I didn't think northern Illinois, the heart of Midwestern cow country, had anything to offer me as far as pristine wilderness was concerned. Then McDowell opened my eyes to a combination of forest, meadow, and savannah rich in an array of bird life from chickadees to owls to egrets and herons and mammals such as possum, coyotes, foxes, and an abundance of white-tailed deer, all on only 515 acres amidst Chicago-land suburbs. So far, McDowell is the only place where I have seen minks in the wild and I consider myself blessed to only live only a quarter-mile south of this pristine forest preserve. During our hike, Sandy and I were talking about deer as we came across their tracks in a muddy creek bed. Then, from out of nowhere, a group of deer showed up in the small meadow we were hiking through. Five or six does were led by one eight-point buck. The buck, in the above photograph, was that buck, the very first McDowell deer I caught on film. For Christmas, I gave my sister a framed print of that deer.

Jogging McDowell

Sunday mornings, people typically go to church. On most Sunday mornings, my cathedral is a 515-acre temple with a church choir of chickadees, red-winged black-birds, tree frogs, and screech and great horned owls. In place of candle-lit altars, and stain glassed windows, are a painter's palate of flowers in spring, summer, and early autumn, and the bright color mosaic of October foliage including the bright red leaves of stag horn sumac, the red and orange leaves of oak and maple, and the yellow and scarlet leaves of assorted trees, shrubs, and bushes. The celestial fire of sunrise, the starry eyes of a possum staring at you from a tree limb, a heron, or egret, silhouetted at the water's edge, and a beaver making a tail-slap on a sunlit lake, are all scriptural lessons of the unspoiled beauty of God's creation. On weekend mornings, and on most other mornings when I'm not working or traveling, dressed in gym clothes, and armed with a small Panasonic digital camera, I am up before dawn, jogging through DuPage County's McDowell Grove Forest Preserve. Fortunately, I actually live half a mile from McDowell's south-ern-most entrance, a wooded area situated between the Spring Meadows Nursing Home and the West Branch of the DuPage River. While I am exercising, in any kind of weather at all seasons of the year, and fighting increment weather and biting insects, I typically jog from the southern-most entrance, across the dam, through the large central savannah, through the small meadow known as the radar field, through the picnic area, across the road bridge, onto the northern-most trail which eventually crosses Ferry Creek and reaches Mud Lake. Then I jog through a forest via a dirt path, return to the main trail, cross Ferry Creek, again, go east bound through the picnic area into some more woods, come out at the northeastern savannah, jog southbound on the east end of the central savannah, back across the dam, then I exit by crossing under the Ogden Avenue bridge and continuing on the Regional Trail, go under the railroad bridge, then leave the trail west-bound to home usually taking Hidden Springs Drive to River Road then Whispering Hills Court.

McDowell Woods is the only place where I have seen minks in the wild. I have never seen a wild mink in Glacier, Yellowstone, the Canadian Rockies, or even Alaska. Yet I have, so far, seen five minks at McDowell. Below is a photo of a tree bridge over Ferry Creek, also something that I have only seen at McDowell. Either it was a fallen tree that was still rooted, and still alive, or a tree that grew horizontally. The bridge washed away in 2012.

McDowell Grove was founded in 1933 as a work camp for the Civilian Conservation Corps work camp and used as a secret radar training school during World War 2. It became a forest preserve in 1946.

WINTER

McDowell Christmas tree
with offspring to your right
Christmas morning 2017

McDowell Christmas tree
Christmas morning 2008

Merry McDowell Christmas!

It was an early, fog-strewn Christmas morning, 2008, at the eastern edge of the central savannah, where I discovered a seven or eight foot fir decorated with lights. The Christmas spirit came to McDowell's snow-blanketed wilderness. Normally, from late November to early February, the tree would be aglow, from dusk through dawn, seen from almost any-where in the central savannah. The tree, apparently, is on the edge of a back yard belonging to one, of many, suburban homes which border McDowell Woods. Snow, especially when it is moon-lit, lights up the landscape so I need no flashlight while jogging during the early morning darkness.

Most white-tailed bucks still have their antlers at least until mid-February, and sometimes until early spring. In general, wildlife is more easily seen, at this time of year, as dark silhouettes in a sea of white. Ice art on riverside tree roots and snow-sprinkled tree canopies are also blessings of beauty in a McDowell winter.

On February 1, 2015, Winter storm Linus dumped several inches of snow on northern Illinois turning McDowell Woods into a snow kingdom making snow art of every tree, shrub, log, rock, forest, meadow, and prairie. I began my jog while it was still dark yet I needed no flashlight to see where I was going. The snow was so fresh and white it seemed to give off its own light. Solitude was at a premium as I saw not a single person for most of my journey. A lone vole darting over a snow-covered trail, and Canada geese and mal-lards huddled along misty river corridors, were the only reminders that I was not on some cold, lifeless planet. I hadn't experienced such a lovely winter since skiing in the Rockies!

THE LOVELY SIDE OF LINUS

SPRING

In April 2013, DuPage County had a flood which severely damaged homes and businesses, closed roads, and, sadly, two people drowned in that flood. Most of McDowell Woods was underwater for well over a week with the Fawell Dam, and the earth-covered dike that follows her eastern border, being the only places where I could jog without getting my feet wet. When the waters subsided, I found trails riddled with ruts and washboards, meadows and savannas with beaten-down grasses and reeds, and forest floors littered with logs, broken limbs and branches, and people's garbage washed in from nearby neighborhoods and streets. In the above-left photo, the posted sign marks where the Regional Trail begins its downward trek under the Ogden Avenue bridge. On the other side of the bridge, the north side, is where you enter McDowell from its southern boundary. Then came the healing process with the first signs of life being my first sighting of Dutchman's Breeches (Dicentra cucullaria), the wildflower on the previous page. While taking photos, I was encircled by a bumblebee the size of a ping pong ball. Apparently, she wanted me out of the way so she could pollinate the blossoms. Only bumblebees have a proboscis long enough for pollinating Dutchman's Breeches. Other signs of spring include two other wildflowers; the trillium, the below left photo, and to its right, two photos of three young white-tailed does celebrating the spring weather after the subsiding floodwaters.

Spring greets me with longer days and an earlier dawn. Before the trees leaf, the understory comes alive with grasses and wildflowers such as the dogtooth violet (above left). I have often seen this flower blossom, on either side of the Regional Trail just north of the small meadow known as the Radar Field. In western Montana, this same wildflower normally has yellow blossoms, and is called the glacier lily because it follows the receding snowline. It is a favorite food of such wildlife as grizzlies, bighorn sheep, mountain goats, and white-tailed and mule deer. Back in Montana, I have eaten the stem and leaves while hiking. White-tailed deer, and other plant-eating wildlife, are all about, feeding on new plant growth. In the Radar Field, the doe, in the above-center photo, let me get within ten feet of her, probably because she was weighed down with pregnancy. Many deer are approachable, at this time of year, but I would advise caution since deer do have strong legs and sharp hooves. People have been killed and injured by deer especially during the May-June fawning season by protective mothers and during the autumn rut by enraged bucks. Nevertheless, I was blessed with seeing every hair on her coat and even her nostril hairs.

Just as beautiful as the sights, of an early McDowell morning, are its sounds. Birds, mostly, such as chickadees, red-winged black birds, cardinals, and buntings echo a symphony, especially in meadows, and savannahs, just as the sparkling eyes of a deer stare back at you while silhouetted on fog-strewn grass. In mid to late April, savannah trees and shrubs flower like a larger-than-life garden in a wide array of colors featuring white, pink, and maroon blossoms. The forest understory, and meadows and savannas, become a painter's palate of wildflowers including the purplish blossoms of iris and spiderwort. Most wildlife have young at this time of year. Not only are large animals like deer protective of their young, but even small animals will confront perceived adversaries many times their size. I learned this, experientially, while jogging through a forest just south of Mud Lake. I was passing two trees, one with a pair of raccoon kits, and the other with their mother, all staring at me. The mother jumped down from the tree, ran toward me for roughly three feet, and stopped, giving me a warning stare. It was my cue to skedaddle as my jog turned into a sprint. During my run, I was alarmed by a loud, high-pitched snarl as I looked to see another adult raccoon scurry up a tree just seven or eight feet to my right. I was breathless and my heart raced for the next three or four minutes. Canada geese are extremely protective of both flock and young at this time of year. If one, or more, hiss at you, heed their warning. Their bites and wing-slaps can cause pain and injury.

Here in McDowell's northeast savanna April is graced with wild plum unfolding in their blossoming white canopies. In May, hawthorn trees blossom with pinkish-white blossoms and June is greeted with the purple blossoms and yellow anthers of iris. Coyotes can be seen, and more often heard, at any time of the year usually in dawn's early light. Quite often, along river corridors, or bordering trees, the purple, white, and pink blossoms of phlox often form their own carpets.

Just as the white and pink flowers paint the dogwoods in spring
beneath a sky of a deep turquoise blue,
like the frosty ribbon cascade that drapes the mountainside

Mother's Day was made for mothers like you

There's something different about where the sun sets that's different from where the sun rises. Where the sun rises shines on what we have today. Where the sun sets promises another tomorrow; which is opportunity, which is possibility.

John Denver

SUMMER

Many a dawn has broken where I have jogged into clouds of ground mist having me think of these fairy tale lands accessible by a beanstalk. I have also seen mist form elongated lines above savannah and meadow. In early to mid June, it hasn't been uncommon for me to find large snapping turtles right by the trail, most likely pregnant mothers. I was amazed at how I could get right up to these snapping turtles for close-up photographs. However, I wasn't about to put a finger or toe in front of the turtle's face and find it missing! Summer continues with more wildflowers coming into bloom such as the purple blossoms of wild bergamot, photographed at sunrise on the previous page. Wild prairie rose, brown-eyed Susan, prairie coneflower, horse nettle, poppies, and butterfly weed are also among the painter's palate of wildflowers.

One Fourth of July morning, before I started bringing my camera with me, I was jogging through the Central Savannah when hot air balloons flew across the horizon. Ahead of me, a young white-tailed doe was also gazing at the balloons. Unfortunately, summer is the season for mosquitoes and biting flies. Before my McDowell pilgrimage, I practically bathe myself in insect repellent and carry the repellent with me. I also wear a visor hat, and netting, both to deter bugs and keep the sun out of my eyes. It was also during the summer that I obtained my fog-graced photos of Bill The Beaver at Mud Lake (inside title page) and a white-tailed doe, and two spotted fawns, on the Regional Trail between the Radar Field and the central savanna.

coyote

Deer   Deer

American Egret

I did not see the deer while taking the photo,
only after seeing the photo on the computer screen

A McDOWELL DRAMA

In the top photo, a white-tailed doe and fawn along the Regional Trail, interrupted from browsing by the flash of my camera. In the bottom photo, the doe faces off a coyote that apparently was stalking them. After this photo was taken, the coyote vanished in the woods.

**McDowell Grove Forest Preserve
Dupage County, Illinois**

faceoff

faceoff

AUTUMN

In September, biting bugs start little wet and late season bloomers, such as goldenrod (yellow) and boneset (white), come into their own. Clear, cool air is conducive to brilliant sunrises and sunsets especially in the later part of the month. It is not uncommon for dark tree canopies to be outlined against red-orange, dusk, and purplish-blue skies, at dawn breaks.

In most of North America, including northern Illinois, October is the month when autumn colors peak. In October 2009, beginning on the 11th, fall colors were changing from day to day. I was on vacation so I was able to jog every morning through McDowell. On the mentioned date, the first frost, and a record low of 28 degrees, turned out to be a photographic blessing because the frost enhanced the color mosaic and was the day that I took some of my best coyote photos. For those who have heard the name, "Coyote Ugly", in McDowell Woods it's "Coyote Handsome"! I did have to remove my gloves to take photos, such as the photo on page 17. Acid-like pain shot through my fingers and my hands turned red and pink. Still, it was worth the near frostbite to capture these moments in time! On October 12,2009, Columbus Day, an over-cast sky brought out the true brilliance of autumn foliage such as what you can see in the black maples and staghorn sumac on this page.

"I wish to speak a word for Nature, for absolute freedom and wildness, as contrasted with a freedom and culture merely civil, to regard man as an inhabitant, or a part and parcel of Nature, rather than a member of society"

Henry David Thoreau

In the shadows of Midwestern Suburbia, a pristine wilderness prevails on little more than 500 acres of forest, meadow, water, and savannah. A misty dawn comes alive as the graceful silhouette of a white-tail bounds through meadow and forest, as her tail flashes like a bouncing lantern. In winter twilight, a noble eight-pointer scans his domain, hundreds of geese dot cold, misty water, and a two firs are lit with Christmas cheer. It's as though I am traveling through scenes on a Hallmark greeting card. In spring, the up-turned white petals, of a fawn lily blossom, are a-glow, with all her brothers and sisters, on a damp forest floor. Beneath the moon-lit dawn sky, a vast savannah comes alive with a symphony of chickadees, cardinals, and red-winged blackbirds. On that same savannah, trees and shrubs of wild plum grace the landscape with a flower menagerie. A starry eyed possum stares back at me from the branches of a small grove and, deep in the forest, a hawthorn canopy, and its maroon and white blossoms, light up the primeval darkness. Meanwhile, a sleek mink stalks the river shoreline for small prey. In the pre-dawn darkness, an owl serenades me and tree frogs seem to make the woodland sing. Despite summer's biting insects, the beauty of wildflower gardens, spotted fawns browsing with their mothers, and a beaver silhouetted in clouds of mist gracing a lake, make this a season of wild blessings. A coyote sings and a great blue heron is silhouetted in sparkling waters. Autumn's color mosaic tops off my wilderness odyssey. The red, scarlet, gold, yellow, pink, and mottled foliage of a wide tree assortment, from oak and maple to hickory, cottonwood, and sumac, form a color mo-saic to make October remembered. Noble bucks have long since shed velvet from antlers and are ready to spar for hinds.

In this wild-land wonder, it is hard to believe that I am still amidst Chicago-land suburbs, just a hop, skip, and a jump from freeways, stores, restaurants, and homes, including mine. Yet I am surrounded by wilderness that would almost rival what I have seen in the Rockies. Nowhere else have I seen a tree bridge and wild minks. In the shadows of Midwestern Suburbia, a wild-land wonder prevails.

JOGGING MCDOWELL PHOTOGRAPHS

(In order of appearance)

Cover Photo: Abraham, the great prince of the McDowell Forest White-tailed buck *Odecoilius Virginianus* Inside cover: white-tailed doe *Odecoilius virginianus* and the West Branch DuPage River Title Page: Bill The Beaver in Mud Lake Beaver *Castor Canadensis* Table of Contents Sarah The Snapping Turtle *Chelydra serpentina* Foreword White-tailed buck 1-Canada Goose Family *Branta canadensis*, Horse Nettle *Solanum carolinense*, White-tailed Doe and Fawns, Wild Prairie Rose *Rosa arkansana suffulta* and Honeybees *Apis Mellifera*, and North America's only marsupial the Opossum *Didelphis virginiana* 2-Tree Bridge over Ferry Creek (Washed away in 2012) and a pair of white-tailed does, beaver-cut tree, Bill The Beaver, The Regional Trail 3-McDowell Christmas Tree Christmas Morning 2008 and McDowell Christmas Tree With Child Christmas Morning 2017 4-McDowell Winter Scenes including a Canada goose congregation, two white-tailed bucks, and Scenes from Winter Storm Linus 5-6-Full page photo of Dutchman's Breeches *Decentra cucullaria,* Above Text: Aftermath of April 2013 Flood, Below Text: Prairie Trillium *Trillium recurvatum recurvatum* three white-tailed does running then stopped 7-Dogtooth Violet *Erythronium cucullaria,* white-tailed doe, and wild plum tree *Prunus   americana*

8-Main Photo-Northeast Hawthorne flowers *latrans* blue flag Iris *Iris* tailed doe on misty *divaricata* in bottom left top right 10-White-tailed River 11-Canada Goose Small photo-White-tailed taken in Central Savanna *Monarda fistulosa*

Savanna in April Small Photos-*Crataegus punctate,* coyote *Canis versicolor* 9-Main Photo-White-morning Small Photos-Phlox *Phlox* photos and dotted hawthorn in does along West Branch DuPage Family framed by picnic pavilion doe and fawns 12-Both photos Right-hand Photo—Wild Bergamot

13-Left-Brown-eyed Susan and wild bergamot in Central Savanna Right-Rocky Raccoon *Procyon lotor* along The Regional Trail 14— The Regional Trail in a misty dawn 15-Butterfly Weed *Asclepias tuberosa*, Brown-eyed Susan *Rudbeckia triloba*, Poppy (Could not find Latin name), Prairie coneflower *Echinacea purpurea* 16-The McDowell Drama: White-tailed family and coyote encounter Interpretive Sign: Great egret *Ardea alba* and white-tailed does in background 17-Coyote in the Central Savanna in October Small Photo-Black Maple branch 18-White-tailed does, goldenrod *Solidago Canadensis,* Tall boneset *Eupatorium altissimum* 19-McDowell in Autumn including Black Maple *Acer nigrum* and staghorn sumac *Rhus typhina* 20-The McDowell Website-A rain sprinkled spider web in the Central Savanna 21-Great blue heron on tree limb and white-tailed deer in the West Branch DuPage River just south of Fawell Dam This page(22)- Bullfrog *Lithobates catesbeianus* in Mud Lake 24-Wild Prairie rose and Honeybees Back Cover-Mud Lake at Dawn

Next page: McDowell's Entrance

Acknowledgements

DuPage County Forest Preserve District: Information and maps

Scott Kobal, Forest Preserve Ecologist: Identification of some of the flora I photographed.

Naperville Library Computer Lab and Their Staff: For their assistance and providing the computers, printers, and low printing costs that made recording and printing possible.

My sister Sandy Manca for introducing me to McDowell.

Two bees or not two bees? That is the question!

GRIZWOLD GRIZZLY

PUBLICATIONS

Printed in the United States
By Bookmasters